This
Book
Belongs
To _

Grolier Enterprises Inc.
SHERMAN TURNPIKE, DANBURY, CONNECTICUT 06816

Book Club Edition

The STORY Of JESUS And The BLIND MAN

An ALICE IN BIBLELAND® Storybook

Written by Alice Joyce Davidson
Illustrated by Victoria Marshall

Text copyright © 1997 by Alice Joyce Davidson
Art copyright © 1997 by The C.R. Gibson Company
Published by The C.R. Gibson Company
Norwalk, Connecticut 06856
Printed in the United States of America
ISBN 0-7667-1734-8

A little girl named Alice
Came home from school one day.
She thought that she would read a bit,
Then later go and play.

She chose her Bible storybook,
Her very favorite one.
And sat down on her round tree bench,
Underneath the sun.

Jesus and the blind man
Was the story that she read,
When suddenly the airmail bird
Swooped down from overhead.

He brought this note to Alice,
Then stayed for just a minute.
As she opened up the envelope,
It had this message in it:

"Reading is the magic key
To take you where you want to be."

Her storybook became a screen.
The screen grew tall and wide,
And Alice took a little walk
To Bibleland inside.

Alice was in Jericho,
And much to her surprise,
The story she was reading
Came to life before her eyes.

She saw a man, all alone
Sitting by a tree.
He told Alice he was blind.
There was nothing he could see.

"Though I can't see the clothes I wear,
Or see my hands or feet,
Or even see my family,
Or people that I meet...

"Though I can't see flowers
Or the blue skies up above,
I know that God is with me—
For I can feel his love."

He had no job. He couldn't work,
Because he couldn't see.
So there was nothing he could do
But beg for charity.

Some people there in Jericho
Would give him coins each day,
While others would avoid him
When they happened by his way.

The blind man wished that he could see
And work like other men,
And never ever have to ask
For charity again.

So he would often say this prayer:

"I thank you, Father, for Your blessings,
that fill my days and nights;
But I would be thankful, still,
If I could have my sight."

People all around him
Were gathering one day.
They said a teacher, Jesus,
Would be stopping by their way.

The blind man knew this was God's Son
And He was good and kind.
He heard Jesus often healed the sick,
And even cured the blind.

"My prayers will all be answered,"
He smiled happily.
"If I can get to Jesus
I'm sure that He will heal me."

The people all were shouting
As Jesus came into view.
And though he couldn't see Him,
The blind man shouted, too.

The crowd grew very quiet
As Jesus started teaching.
But the blind man kept on shouting
As Jesus started preaching.

The people tried to quiet him,
But he yelled so noisily,
"Jesus, Master, Healer,
Have pity, please, on me."

"Shush, now," someone told him.
"Jesus has come to teach.
He doesn't want to hear you
As you holler and you screech."

But he shouted even louder,
And he fell down on his knees,
"Jesus, Master, hear me,
Will you help me, please?"

When Jesus heard him shouting,
He said, "Come over here."
The man stood up, then faithfully,
Walked and drew quite near.

"What do you want?" asked Jesus.
"What do you want of me?"
"Master," said the blind man,
"I only want to see.

"I want to see God's flowers,
The sun that shines above,
And all the wondrous gifts God made
And gave to us with love."

"Your faith has healed you," Jesus said.
"You see the sun shine bright."
The man cried, "Thank you, thank you, Jesus,
For giving me my sight!"

Then the man recited
A special heartfelt prayer
To thank God for His mercy,
His goodness and His care.

The time had come for Alice
To leave that Bible scene.
She came back home from Bibleland
By walking through her screen.

As Alice went inside her house,
And put her book away,
She thought about the lesson
From her storybook that day.

The blind man knew his Master.
His faith was pure and right.
Jesus blessed him with a miracle
And he regained his sight.

"We, too, can have rich blessings
If we trust in God above.
He'll see our faith, and He in turn
Will bless us with His love."